MY Grief Observed

William E. Johnson

Copyright © 2015 William E. Johnson

All rights reserved.

ISBN: 1514291444
ISBN-13: 978-1514291443

Scripture references taken from:

The New King James Version®. Copyright © 1982 by Thomas Nelson. Used by permission. All rights reserved.
and
THE HOLY BIBLE, NEW INTERNATIONAL VERSION®, NIV® Copyright © 1973, 1978, 1984, 2011 by Biblica, Inc.® Used by permission. All rights reserved worldwide.
and
The Authorized (King James) Version. Rights in the Authorized Version in the United Kingdom are vested in the Crown. Reproduced by permission of the Crown's patentee, Cambridge University Press.

DEDICATION

For Amy, Joshua, Allison and Jericho
and
in loving memory of Beth.

CONTENTS

STEALING FROM CLIVE 3

SHE WILL DIE 8

SHE'S IN A BETTER PLACE 17

I BELIEVE 21

I HURT 26

I WONDER 33

I LEARN 39

I AM THANKFUL 45

I PRAY 50

I CONTINUE 54

ADDENDUM 57

ABOUT THE AUTHOR 61

ACKNOWLEDGMENTS

It is with heartfelt thanks that I acknowledge the contributions of several dear brothers and sisters. Dr. Charles Whitfield, my mentor and friend, Rev. Jerry Boritzki, Rev. Don Davies, Sister Carolyn Davies, Dr. John T. Cornette, Brother Steve Oswald, Brother Bob Davis, and Sister Christina Davis. Your comments and suggestions were so helpful.

And of course, the contributions, prayers, and help from Amy Johnson, Joshua Johnson and Allison Johnson were priceless.

Most of all, I wish to give praise and thanks to my Savior, Jesus Christ, Who has brought me through this, and continues to bring me through.

To God be the glory. Great things He hath done.

STEALING FROM CLIVE

That which has been is what will be, That which is done is what will be done, And there is nothing new under the sun. (Ecclesiastes 1:9)

On September 18th, my wife died. It was sudden. There had been no warning. Beth was healthy and happy one minute, and the next she was gone. A week later I sat down in my empty house for the first time, post funeral. The frenetic activity of the days since her death had been all that occupied my mind, but now that was over. And there, in the silence of that once-so-joyful home, the realization came crashing over me like breakers.

She had died.

She was dead.

She was gone.

I looked across the quiet room at the empty chair where she had so recently sat. Grief crushed me. Tears fell. I have never felt more alone.

People handle grief in different ways, I'm told. Well, as a reader, my first efforts at handling my grief involved reading. And as a Christian and a pastor, the first place I looked was God's Book, the Bible. So I opened that best-of-all-books to the Psalms. Countless times I had counseled others during times of grief, assuring them that the Psalms would bring comfort and clarity.

Cast your burden on the LORD, And He shall sustain you; He shall never permit the righteous to be moved. (Psalms 55:22)

Truly my soul silently waits for God; From Him comes my

salvation. He only is my rock and my salvation; He is my defense; I shall not be greatly moved. (Psalms 62:1-2)

Wait on the LORD: be of good courage, and he shall strengthen thine heart: wait, I say, on the LORD. (Psalm 27:14)

For his anger endureth but a moment; in his favour is life: weeping may endure for a night, but joy cometh in the morning. (Psalm 30:5)

In the days following Beth's death a dear sister shared a verse from Lamentations which encouraged me perhaps more than any other. *Though He causes grief, Yet He will show compassion According to the multitude of His mercies. (Lamentations 3:32)*

I found comfort in such passages. And I also found it in the gospels. It seems when I most need, I most need Jesus Himself, and so I turned to the accounts about Him... His Words... His miracles... Him.

And as I took in the inspired words of Scripture, I found that my many attempts at counseling others had not been totally off the mark. The psalms... the gospels... God's Word... it all did, indeed, provide comfort and strength and clarity during my grieving process.

But... as I mentioned... I'm a reader, and as a reader, I didn't stop with the Bible.

I turned to my library of books, and pulled several down

that sounded like they might assuage my grief. As I surveyed the collection, I couldn't help but see the little offering by C.S. Lewis, simply entitled "A Grief Observed." It was beckoning to me from the stack. Well, I had been meaning to read that little book for years anyway, and now seemed a better time than ever.

So I read it. And I wept along with Lewis. He, too, had lost his wife, Joy, and this little book was a journal of his thoughts and experiences arising from that devastating loss. As he journaled his grief process, I empathized, for the mutuality of pain was not dimmed by the ocean that separated Lewis' reality and mine. Nor did his experiences as an Englishman differ from mine as an American. Even the half century of time that stood between Joy's death and Beth's made no difference. The pain of his loss mirrored in so many ways the pain of mine.

I found myself wishing I had the discipline and ability to journal my grief, as Lewis did. I even tried a couple times, but found myself stopping and starting and eventually giving up. But after some time passed, I found myself able to think about the loss... the process... the pain... and write about it. This little booklet was born out of that effort.

Lewis's booklet is not a theological treatise. It is not a Bible study to assist one in understanding Biblical truth about death and loss. It is not particularly Biblical at all, but rather provides a running commentary on the affect his loss had on him. It is a glimpse into a sorrowing and wounded believer's heart and soul, and as such it helped me immensely because I could empathize with him. My goal with this booklet is to provide something similar - not a Bible study or theological understanding of death and dying. Rather I hope this booklet will simply share some thoughts and observations from the heart of someone who deeply loves the Lord, and deeply loved one whom the Lord has taken home. It is not meant to be a study in grief. It is meant to be a picture of grief, and the results thereof.

So, with apologies to and thanks to C.S. Lewis, I share MY Grief Observed. I pray it helps others as they observe their's.

SHE WILL DIE

... it is appointed for men to die... (Hebrews 9:27)

Man who is born of woman is of few days... (Job 14:1)

The righteous perish, and no one takes it to heart; the devout are taken away, and no one understands that the righteous are taken away to be spared from evil. Those who walk uprightly enter into peace; they find rest as they lie in death. (Isaiah 57:1-2)

The day before had been such a good day. We were nearing the end of a week long vacation out of state, one of the best vacations we remembered enjoying together. While our vacations often included other family members, this one had been specifically planned to be us... just the two of us. And it had exceeded our expectations, as we enjoyed several wonderful days of quiet joy together.

The last day was especially sweet, starting with breakfast, a bit of shopping, a hike through a breathtakingly beautiful nature preserve, and finally one last site-seeing visit to an area mansion. Touring old homes was something we loved doing together, and so we rounded out the afternoon with that tour before we headed back toward our lodgings and dinner.

Beth had barbecue ribs for dinner. I don't know why I remember that detail, but I do. I wish I could remember whether she ordered dessert. It would give me joy to remember her last meal including dessert.

We returned to our room. We watched a movie together - a comedy. I'm thankful that one of my last memories of Beth is her laugh.

I turned out the lights, and we slept, until I was awakened early the next morning by the sounds of very erratic breathing. I don't remember the exact time. I tried to wake her, but I could not and within just a few seconds she stopped breathing completely. Frantic, I called 911. The 911 operator had me move her to the floor and start CPR. To the very best of my ability I performed CPR on her for about 5 minutes before the local sheriff arrived. He then took over and continued CPR. The EMTs arrived after another 5 minutes and performed more CPR. They also put a tube down her throat and administered some sort of chemical inducements which finally got her heart started again. By this time, she had not drawn a single breath on her own for 15 minutes, nor had her heart beat without the aid of CPR for 15 minutes. I watched helplessly as the EMT technicians wheeled her to the ambulance. I stood there in the parking lot in my pajamas, reeling from the shock of it all, and trying desperately to understand their directions concerning how to get to the hospital. The lights came on atop the ambulance, and they were gone.

Sprinting back into the room, I threw on some clothes, and drove as quickly as possible to the hospital. By the time I got there Beth was already surrounded by an army of doctors and nurses. I could not even see her through the crowd of people. I was shown to a waiting room and assured someone would be with me shortly.

At 8:35, I spoke with the attending physician. "Your wife was experiencing ventricular fibrillation when she came in. We have her on 2 very powerful meds to keep her pressure up," he told me. He then took me to meet the cardiologist who was working with Beth. I still could not get into the room with her to see her.

The cardiologist informed me that she was having a major heart attack but he was unsure what had caused it. At this point, he thought it might be a stroke or it might have been a problem with the heart, itself. He had ordered a cat scan of her brain and possibly a heart catheterization as the next steps.

It was now 9:00, and I was taken to a waiting area near the cat scan. The doctors assured me that they would come to meet me there after the tests were completed.

Ten minutes passed, and then the doctor returned to share the results of the cat scan. It was not good news. The scan revealed a brain bleed. This caused the doctors to believe that she did not actually have a heart attack but rather the heart stopped, probably as a result of the bleed causing her to stop breathing. The doctors left to consult on whether to transfer her to another hospital.

At 10:20, I watched as they wheeled her into a helicopter and transported her to a large hospital better equipped to handle this condition. As I was leaving the hospital, the doctors told me that there was a possibility the bleed could be relieved and her condition would improve. The helicopter would take 15 minutes to make it to the second hospital. I jumped into my car and drove. It took me an hour - one of the longest hours of my life.

At 11:41 I arrived and learned that the neurosurgeon

had already been with Beth, and I was told to wait for him. At 12:05 I was taken to the room where Beth lay peacefully on the bed, completely surrounded by IV drips and tubes. She was on a ventilator. She could not breathe on her own. Her heart was only beating with the aid of the IV drugs pumping into her.

I wept, for about the hundredth time that day.

The neurosurgeon walked into the room and saw me, and immediately asked me to follow him. He took me to a consultation room and spoke several sentences which I will hear in my mind forever.

"She is in deep coma with little to no blood getting to her brain."

"She has no lower brain functions at all."

"She will not recover from this."

"She will die."

For several seconds I could not respond to this news. A strangling sensation came over me and I was completely unable to speak. I recall gasping... trying to breathe. I recall huge wracking sobs that escaped me no matter how I tried to hold them back. I asked how long I still had with her, and the doctor said he did not know but he would have her made comfortable and maintained until the family arrived.

My two children were both adults, and living on their

own. I had contacted them, of course, when the initial collapse occurred, but I had not kept them fully informed as the day went along. I had told them it was serious and they needed to come, but I didn't want them rushing and putting themselves in danger, so I held back the full details. I now contacted my daughter and was told they were enroute. "Hurry," I whispered into the phone. It was 1:00 in the afternoon.

I sat alone in the room with my wife for the next four hours - watching the machines operate her lungs and heart, talking to her and hoping against hope that she could hear me. I so wanted to see some movement... some sign... something that would say "I hear you, Baby." But there was nothing. Only the steady hum and hiss of machinery and the beeping of the multiple IV machines feeding chemicals into her bloodstream.

There were so many things unsaid. As I looked at her lifeless face, I knew that even though she had not yet been pronounced dead, she was with the Lord. I knew she was no longer with me in the room. But I spoke to her anyway. I held her hand. I kissed her. I stroked her hair. Every second was beyond precious, even though I knew she was gone.

Later that afternoon, the doctor visited again. He showed me scans of her brain and stressed that this was a catastrophic sub arachnoid hemorrhage and that the brain had swelled to the point that no blood vessels can even be seen on the images. He provided another sentence then that I will never forget, pointing out that her condition was "incompatible with life." He could not declare her dead yet, though he believed she was in that state. There were protocols to be followed, and it would take until the next day before they could be completed. Her official time of death could not, therefore, be called until those protocols were completed.

The doctor left me alone in the room with her. The family was still three and a half hours away. The loneliest day I've ever experienced dragged on.

It was 9:00 that evening when the kids finally arrived and learned the full extent of the situation. I have had to say some hard things to people at times. I have had to deliver hard news to my children. But I have never had to say anything that was as difficult as when I had to say to them, "Mom is not coming home."

The next day was a slow march toward that inevitable moment when the doctor would confirm what I already knew. Beth was dead. The official time of death was 12:12 PM on September 19, but in my heart I will always know the Lord took her from my arms on the morning of September 18, when I awoke to her last breath.

Each of the children spent some private time alone with her, and then I spent my last moment with my soul mate. I kissed her forehead one last time. I held her hand one last time. I told her I would love her forever, one last time.

As I turned and walked from that room, walking away from the love of my life and everything I had known for my entire adult existence, I reflected back on the thirty-five years I had spent with this beautiful woman. Thirty five years earlier, she and I had gone to a jewelry store and purchased our wedding bands. Etched inside those bands was Psalm 34:3 - "Oh, magnify the LORD with me, and let us exalt His name together." My mind traced through the ensuing thirty five years. Many ups and downs. But we had, indeed, tried to magnify Him together. For some reason, God had decided to call a halt to that togetherness, and called her home.

I tried to remember the words to that beautiful chorus that I had recited at so many funerals:

But just think of stepping on shore
And finding it heaven,
Of touching a hand
And finding it God's,
Of breathing the air
And finding it celestial,
Of waking up in Glory
And finding it home.

I did rejoice for her, knowing she was with her Lord. But as I walked away I knew I now had to magnify the Lord without her... alone. I had never been alone. I feared. I knew in my heart that a wonderful reunion day would come, but the salty taste of my tears reminded me that this was not that day.

This was a terrible day.

I grieved.

SHE'S IN A BETTER PLACE

But I do not want you to be ignorant, brethren, concerning those who have fallen asleep, lest you sorrow as others who have no hope. (1 Thessalonians 4:13)

Precious in the sight of the LORD is the death of His saints. (Psalms 116:15)

Having sat with and stood beside so many in this situation, I was surprised at how hard this ordeal was. Sitting with somebody else who has lost a love, and being yourself the one with the loss… well those are two very different things, indeed.

We sat around the little table in the funeral home office, and chose colors and casket and vault and options and flowers and service details. Even though this was a proceeding I had participated in before in support of others, and even though my two grown children were there beside me now, I had to excuse myself on a couple of occasions when the raw emotion of the moment would take over. This was something I had always known might be in my future. But this was the present. It was too soon. I couldn't begin to get my mind around the task of choosing a casket. And the visit to the cemetery to select burial plot locations was horrible. I wept for a long time after that experience.

But soon the preparations were made and the day arrived. There were 2 hours set aside for the viewing, with the funeral planned for the following day. The family was to arrive an hour before the scheduled viewing, for a private time. But we had not been there 15 minutes before guests began to arrive. They were admitted, and the calling hours thus began almost an hour before scheduled. A steady stream of mourners poured into the funeral home for the next 4 hours, with the line extending well into the street and around the building much of the evening.

My memory of those 4 hours is not very clear. I remember lots of hugs and buckets of tears. I recall many taking me by the hand and sharing words of comfort with me. And I have a vague recollection of my daughter, son, and daughter in law standing with me. But my overriding memory is one of thankfulness. Her life had touched so many, and now in these final moments there was such an outpouring of memory and love and support in recognition of that. I knew she no longer needed that affirmation, but I did, and was thankful to see it. I needed, more than at any other time, to know that she mattered. And seeing the crowd, and hearing of the influence from her life on so many, I was thankful to know that she had.

A lot of pastors came through the line that day. So too, a lot of friends and family members, many of whom I had not seen in years. Some lived very nearby but due to the busyness of life were seldom part of mine. Some were from the distant past, and I was surprised to see them when such a chasm of time had grown between us. And of course, some came through the line that day who might better have stayed home. There were those who had been unkind or difficult in life, now appearing after her death in some feigned display of concern. Those I wanted to punch dead in the face. I confess that in spite of my grief and tenderness, the sight of some such were enough to bring a vengeful spirit to the fore. Forgive me for that, Lord.

Of course, there were the words. Most had something

to say. Over and over the same words. "I'm sorry for your loss." "She's in a better place." "She's better off now." "You will see her again." "To be absent from the body is to be present with the Lord."

I knew these things were true. And I nodded and smiled each time I heard them. "I know, and thank you," was my response more times than I could count.

I BELIEVE

For this reason I also suffer these things; nevertheless I am not ashamed, for I know whom I have believed and am persuaded that He is able to keep what I have committed to Him until that Day. (2 Timothy 1:12)

... being confident of this very thing, that He who has begun a good work in you will complete it until the day of Jesus Christ... (Philippians 1:6)

You never know how much you really believe anything until its truth or falsehood becomes a matter of life and death to you.[1]

Never doubt in the darkness what God has shown you in the light. (Unknown)

---

[1]Lewis, C.S., "A Grief Observed"

If I were to step outside myself for a minute and observe this experience as an outsider, the thing I would find most interesting is the effect all this had on my faith. I don't suppose anybody can go through such an experience without questions surfacing. "Why, God?" was one that intruded on my thoughts often. And it certainly wasn't the only question that I had during these days of grief. But one of the things I found interesting, and indeed encouraging, was that in spite of the questions, my faith did not waiver.

I believed before this happened. I believed throughout the experience. And now, as I look back on it after time has passed, I still believe. And that gives me joy. It gives me peace. It gives me hope. It encourages my soul perhaps more than anything else that has resulted from losing Beth. In spite of it all, I find that I still believe.

I have been a follower of Jesus Christ for more than 40 years, having been saved at the age of 12. Actually, I walked an aisle in the very church I now serve in as pastor, and prayed to my newly accepted Savior on May 3, 1970. I always remember that date because it was one day before the famous riot at Kent State University.

During the more than four decades of my Christian walk, I have seen many believers experience trial and pain and grief. Some have stood. Others have not. It seems the road behind me is littered with the memories of those who seemed so strong and then were hewed to the ground by some pain or difficulty. I know that many times in the past I've pondered what my response would be to such an event. And here I was, in the aftermath of just such an event, and I was finding that my response was one of faith. I still believed. I claim no credit for this, of course. I know it is just another reminder of the grace of God alive and well in my life. But it nonetheless comforted and comforts me to know it was there... working... staying... enduring.

I suppose this was such a pleasant surprise to me because of the general blessing which God had bestowed on me. Up until recently, my life had been largely devoid of pain. Where many people suffer throughout their lives, and are quite familiar with how their faith holds up under trial, I was the opposite. The majority of my life to date having been pain free, trouble free, and need free, I had often wondered how I would respond if "the bill ever came due."

I thought back to the brutal experience of my son's cancer. That was the first major test.

I had been hunting in southern Ohio, my back against a tree and my longbow across my lap, when my cell phone buzzed. I looked at the display and saw my wife's name there. "She knows I'm hunting and so this must be important, or she wouldn't have interrupted the hunt," I thought. I answered the phone and heard words that are forever in my memory - "You need to come home right now. Joshua has cancer." And so a year long ordeal began. Surgeries and chemotherapy...

hospital visits every day. We prayed. Our church prayed. Complications came and there was a day when Beth and I kissed Joshua's almost lifeless face and walked from the room, honestly believing we had kissed him goodbye. I recall arriving back home after that visit, walking into our backyard and sitting together on a wooden swing. We wept in each other's arms.

But our faith remained. At no point during that horrible ordeal did Beth seem to stop believing. Neither did I.

And now I had experienced what must surely be the ultimate loss in saying goodbye to my beautiful wife. A pastor friend visited me in my home a few days after Beth's death, and he tried to comfort and encourage me by reminding me that there is no greater relationship on earth than the one between husband and wife. He quoted from *Genesis 2:24* and pointed out that marriage is the only relationship where the Bible says that the parties become one flesh. Only in marriage do the two become one. And my pastor friend pointed out that there is no greater loss than the loss of a spouse, where the whole is taken away. "Two become ONE in marriage," he said, "and when one of the two dies, the ONE is taken away."

AND YET I find my faith unshaken, and I marvel at that. I am humbly reminded that God saved me and God keeps me... that God opened my heart to faith in the first place, and God keeps me believing. All is of grace, and grace alone.

I discovered through my grief that this is a silver lining in such an experience - it provides evidence that shouts the reality of faith... my faith. In spite of the pain, the loss, the loneliness, the tears, and the fear - I STILL BELIEVE.

A few years ago, gospel artist Steven Curtis Chapman, and his wife Mary Beth Chapman shared the terrible tragedy of their 17 year old son accidentally running over their 5 year old daughter in the driveway. Sometime thereafter, they were interviewed by Larry King on his Larry King Live TV show. At the conclusion of that interview Larry King asked, "Mary Beth, Did you ever question your belief?" Mary Beth answered, "Never. Never. You know what, I tell my closest friends - when it got to the darkest, darkest point, and we went as far down as we could. We might not even have landed feet up... we might have landed right on our face. But the foundation was solid. And it was there. And we landed and it's a day at a time."[2]

Only in Christ do we find such resources! Only in Christ is there such a firm foundation that helps us believe even through pain. And I praise God for that.

---

[2] "Tragic Accident Tests Faith", CNN - The Larry King Live Show,
http://www.cnn.com/TRANSCRIPTS/0808/07/lkl.01.html

I HURT

Talk to me about the truth of religion and I'll listen gladly. Talk to me about the duty of religion and I'll listen submissively. But don't come talking to me about the consolations of religion or I shall suspect that you don't understand.[3]

So Sarah died in Kirjath Arba (that is, Hebron) in the land of Canaan, and Abraham came to mourn for Sarah and to weep for her. (Genesis 23:2)

---

[3]Lewis, C.S., "A Grief Observed"

It was on December 18, 3 months to the day from her death, that I came across that verse from Genesis in my daily Bible reading. Three months had passed, and I still mourned for Beth, and wept for her. I still hurt.

"She will not recover from this. She will die." I cannot forget the incredible pain those words brought to me when the doctor spoke them. I cannot deny that at that moment, I hurt, and I hurt terribly.

"Your mom is not coming home." Telling my kids that their beloved mother was gone was one of the most painful things I've ever done. As I tried to get those words out, all the while seeing the sorrow and pain in their eyes, I felt pain. I hurt along with them.

As a pastor of a church, it's just part of the territory that people talk and gossip about you. We were not even close to knowing whether Beth would live or die yet when false accounts and inaccurate details had already exploded across social media pronouncing that she was dead. When it became known, for a fact, that she was indeed gone, I knew I had to tell family, friends, and church members the real story. That announcement was yet another source of pain. It seemed so final when I saw the words typed out on my computer screen. As I told the world, the pain washed over me.

And since the doctor had certain protocols to follow before he could make the pronouncement of death, I found myself sleeping on a little pull out bed next to

Beth's. I believed she was gone. Every indication was that she was gone, and yet I had to wait for that final pronouncement. And there are no words to describe the sadness I felt during that vigil.

Beth had chosen during life to donate her organs after death. The initial conversations with the doctor about this were hard, but the meeting where my children and I were given the details about that process was even more so. I listened nearly unable to speak as the nurse and doctor described how they would harvest parts of my beloved wife's body. I knew she had wanted it, and so I sat there mute, unable to object throughout the description. It was a profound relief when my son spoke up and indicated that he was not comfortable with some of the steps they wished to take. There was only so much desecration of her body that any of us could take. We were and are thrilled that she was able to help others even in her death, but the pain of knowing what that gift required be done to her body... well it hurt to contemplate.

I knew the theology of the thing. I knew that body was no longer her. I know that we are not our bodies, but rather "we wear our bodies" as one pastor friend put it. And she was no longer wearing hers, but had taken up residence in heaven awaiting that day when she would receive her glorified body. But that didn't change the fact that when I looked at that body I saw her. And anything that was done to that body felt to me like it was being done to her.

At one point the doctor entered the room and began the process of drawing blood from her arm. This, of course, required another needle stick. I asked him to stop. "Why do you need to stick her again," I asked with tears welling in my eyes. "She hated needles. I don't want any more needles put in her." He looked at me somewhat confused and reminded me that she was gone. "There is no further feeling or pain," he said. But it didn't matter. I knew that body wasn't her, but I FELT like it was, and it hurt terribly to think of any further suffering being inflicted upon her.

There are just so many aspects of the experience that were sources of terrible pain... terrible hurt. I'll never forget that last kiss - leaning over her quiet body, breathing only with the aid of a machine, and tenderly kissing her forehead... her face... her lips... one last time. And then walking away, knowing that it was the last time. And the long drive home with my daughter, both of us weeping most of the way home.

And I will never forget the trauma of the first viewing at the funeral home. Seeing her body lying in a casket was almost indescribably painful. I don't recall anything else in my life that has drawn such uncontrollable wracking sobs from me.

There is no doubt that pain, sorrow, and hurt have been emotions I've experienced constantly since God called her home. It comes in waves. For a period of time I may seem to have my emotions in check, and then a song or a word or a place or a memory will surface and the waves will crash over me and the tears will come. Firsts have been terrible triggers of such pain. The first Thanksgiving I couldn't even pray with the family over the meal. The tears prevented it. The first Christmas hurt terribly, as did every other first - the first anniversary alone... her first birthday without her there... the first birthday of the grandchild she had loved so much.

And the reality that God drove home to me and continues to drive home to me is that pain is real. Hurt is real. Sorrow and loss HURT! I don't think I'll ever counsel people quite the same way as I did before. At least I hope I won't. In the past there had always been a thought in the back of my mind that when someone was suffering from such pain at a loss, it was in some way an indication that their faith was lacking. If they believed their loved one was in a better place, why were they crying so? But now it was me. And I knew I believed. And I still hurt.

As I thought about this truth, I couldn't help but think of Jesus and His dear friend Lazarus. Lazarus had two sisters, Mary and Martha. One day Jesus received word that Lazarus was sick, and so He went to visit. Before Jesus arrived, though, Lazarus died and was buried. Several times during my grieving process, I read the story:

So when Jesus came, He found that he had already been

in the tomb four days. And many of the Jews had joined the women around Martha and Mary, to comfort them concerning their brother. Now Martha, as soon as she heard that Jesus was coming, went and met Him, but Mary was sitting in the house. Now Martha said to Jesus, "Lord, if You had been here, my brother would not have died. But even now I know that whatever You ask of God, God will give You." Jesus said to her, "Your brother will rise again." Martha said to Him, "I know that he will rise again in the resurrection at the last day." Jesus said to her, "I am the resurrection and the life. He who believes in Me, though he may die, he shall live. And whoever lives and believes in Me shall never die. Do you believe this?" She said to Him, "Yes, Lord, I believe that You are the Christ, the Son of God, who is to come into the world." Then, when Mary came where Jesus was, and saw Him, she fell down at His feet, saying to Him, "Lord, if You had been here, my brother would not have died." Therefore, when Jesus saw her weeping, and the Jews who came with her weeping, He groaned in the spirit and was troubled. And He said, "Where have you laid him?" They said to Him, "Lord, come and see." Jesus wept. (John 11:17, 19-27, 32-35)

As I read this story, I couldn't escape the incongruous fact that moments after Jesus' cheeks glistened with His tears, He miraculously raised Lazarus from the dead. Here He was, knowing that death was defeated, and that within minutes He would restore Lazarus to life, and yet He wept. A new understanding of this scene dawned on me. Jesus wept because death is painful. He wept because it is an enemy. He wept because he saw the pain in the eyes of His friends. He wept because it HURT.

Jesus wept... and in His weeping I found permission to weep at my loss. It didn't mean I believed any less. It just meant that the experience hurt.

I WONDER

I've asked a lot of questions since my love died. I wonder about a lot of things.

For example, I wonder what she is seeing now... what she is doing now... what her days are like. As a Bible believing Christian, I believe that when her eyes closed in death here, they opened in the very presence of Jesus Christ, where she will live in peace and prosperity and health and happiness forever. "Absent from the body, present with the Lord," as the Apostle Paul put it. But what must that be like? I confess that when I allow my mind to wander into this realm, there is no sorrow accompanying the thoughts, for it is a wonderful thing to contemplate.

My wife was hard of hearing. I know she has perfect hearing now. What must that be like for her?

My sweetheart suffered from some things that caused her pain. I know there is no such thing as pain where she is now. What must that be like?

She had started to slow down a bit as she entered the second half of life. She didn't have quite the same spring in her step that she had had when I first knew her. Now - she is living where the One Who makes all things new has given her newness of life and newness of everything. What must that be like?

It must be wonderful!

I can only imagine what it will be like
When I walk by Your side
I can only imagine what my eyes will see
When Your face is before me
I can only imagine

Surrounded by Your glory
What will my heart feel
Will I dance for You Jesus
Or in awe of You be still
Will I stand in Your presence
Or to my knees will I fall
Will I sing hallelujah
Will I be able to speak at all
I can only imagine
I can only imagine.[4]

I wonder at a lot of things since God called her home. Some of them bring me pain and confusion. This one brings me joy, and when I find myself running over speed bumps of sorrow, I try hard to think about this one - I wonder what she is seeing now?

---

[4] *Kipley, Pete, "I Can Only Imagine", Songs From The Indigo Room, Wordspring Music LLC*

I wonder about other things, though, too. A lot of things happened during the grieving process, and I can't help but wonder about some of them.

For example, I wonder how I totally missed how much I depended on her. Her mind - how did I not see it's influence on mine? I find it so hard to make the simplest decision now, for I took it for granted that she would always be beside me working through decisions - together. How did I so miss the import of her intelligence in my life?

I wonder why I have a need to visit the cemetery. I recall some years ago when I used to be heavily into bicycling. I would often ride many miles in a day, and one of the routes often travelled took me past a cemetery. There was a lady who was often seated next to a headstone, working on needlepoint, or crocheting. I remember being somewhat judgmental of her. "If she were a believer, she would know that her loved one is not there, but rather with the Lord." I am ashamed now at how I thought about her, because for some reason now I need to go to the cemetery. I know she is not there, but yet that grave is a connection, and one that I cherish. I wonder why it is, that in spite of all I know about the Biblical teaching on death and resurrection... all I understand about the fact she is with Christ in heaven... I need to visit that grave.

My mind wanders to the days of the funeral itself, and I find myself wondering why those I expected to be there weren't... and why those I would never have expected to be there were. Some of the most vocal and outspoken professors of Christ were nowhere to be found when I needed them, and some that had so loudly proclaimed their friendship to my wife and I in the past became no-shows. That group included a good number of people into whose lives Beth and I had poured ours... into whose sufferings we had entered, and now that the circumstances were reversed, their support for us was absent. But some whom I would never have expected found resources of comfort and encouragement to share with me. I wondered about that, and prayed I would never again be in the first group (for I think perhaps I have been before), and would always and ever be in the latter group.

I also wondered why the very things I always say at funerals rang so hollow. This was the funeral of a pastor's wife. Fellow pastors and their wives came out of the woodwork. It seemed every other person that walked through the receiving line that terrible evening was a pastor. And almost all of them said the things I would have said. "Brother, we can rejoice knowing that she is not here, but is with the Lord." "Absent from the body and present with the Lord." "Brother, we sorrow not as those with no hope." Verse after verse and platitude after platitude... all things I had said before.

I cannot and will not fault these brothers for their honest and godly efforts to comfort my broken heart. But as I heard the words coming to me rather than from me, I was shocked at their ineffectiveness. They weren't helping me. And I wondered at that.

Words didn't help me much at all, as a matter of fact. What did help were the hugs and the tears. I wondered why for someone like me, who is not by nature a "hugger", what really helped the most were those hugs... those tears. I noticed one dear friend approaching in the receiving line that evening. He had been in our wedding. We had been friends all our lives. Suddenly he stood before me and the tears were dripping down his cheeks. He threw his arms around my neck and just sobbed my name. No other words. Just that hug, and those tears, and then he was gone. I wondered why nothing that was said that evening helped as much as that, and I determined to talk less to those in pain, and weep with them more. Why did it take such pain in my life to help me understand the Biblical imperative to "weep with those who weep?"

And there is another thing I wondered about. And it brought me shame. I was back at my work place some weeks after the funeral when Sandy walked into my office with tears on her face. "I haven't been able to work up the strength to walk in here and tell you how sorry I am for your loss," she wept. She went on to describe the pain and sorrow she had suffered when her husband had died recently. She knew what I felt and wanted me to know she was praying for me and hurting with me. I thanked her and she left my office. I wept.

But my tears were because of my own heartlessness, and not because of her concern. I was ashamed to admit that I had not even known of her husband's death. I worked with this woman. Her office was only a couple doors away from mine. I wondered with shame why I had been so oblivious to her suffering. Why had I not done anything to show concern when she was hurting? I wondered then and wonder now how I could be so unaware of how desperately hurting other people are. And I pray for forgiveness for a callous heart, and ask for awareness of the hurt in others. I wonder if maybe that isn't a good thing that has sprung from this terrible loss.

I LEARN

"Experience: that most brutal of teachers. But you learn, my God do you learn." ~ *C. S. Lewis*

Everything about this life is merely preparation for eternity. I've believed and preached that most of my life. And so in the midst of grief, there has always been the thought, "What is God teaching me in this? What does He want me to learn?" And, brutal as some of the lessons have been, I have learned some things... or at least been reminded of some things:

Death is unexpected, no matter how ready you are. There's no way to plan for death. I thought Beth and I had things pretty well in order. Life insurance was in place, wills were on file, and conversations had been held concerning important decisions.

But I WASN'T ready. It was a total shock, as if I had never given it a moment's thought.

Things can change in an instant. Anybody who has heard me preach knows that I believe this, and always have. I warn people and plead with people in nearly every sermon. "You do not know whether you have tomorrow. You need to trust Christ right now, because you have no guarantee of any future opportunity." But nothing quite drives home the point like watching your beautiful wife smiling and laughing before bed, and then waking to the sounds of her dying - perfectly healthy one minute and with the Lord the next.

We had so many plans for the future. I knew it was a possibility that one of us would die suddenly, but I never really gave it enough thought.

This experience has reminded me that I simply do not have tomorrow. I cannot count on it. My times are in His hands, and my steps are ordered by the Lord - just as were the times and steps of my beautiful wife. *A man's heart plans his way, But the LORD directs his steps. (Proverbs 16:9)* I pray this reminder causes me to be more urgent in my service... more aware of the passing of each minute... less prone to diddle with the work of God and the people of God.

I need to concentrate on the eternal. Yes, I've preached this truth, too. But watching everything about the now get pulled out from under you in a split second has a marvelous way of crystalizing your thoughts, and narrowing your focus. Everything about my future plans on this earth was smashed to pieces with that one rasping final breath. Nothing was left of all we had planned for.

But the eternal is still there, and always should have been my main focus. I pray that this reminder stays with me, and that my life remains focused now on that which cannot die.

Mourning the loss of a spouse has multiple dimensions. I find myself missing HER so much that I cannot breathe. But at other times I find myself missing IT just as much. And by IT I mean the generic aspects of it - female companionship... female conversation... female laughter. And when that aspect of the mourning comes to the fore, it is coupled with guilt. How can I mourn anything but HER?

I'm still working on this lesson, and asking God to teach me through it. But I have certainly learned to be less judgmental of those who are struggling through loss like this. The emotions are not simple... they are multidimensional and difficult to work through.

People don't know how to deal with death. I think the thing that has surprised me the most is how no one talks about her. And the people that have been the biggest blessing to me are the ones who use her name and do talk about her. I would no doubt have been in the former category before, but I'm determined to learn this lesson. Hearing her name does not hurt, it helps. Having a brother or sister acknowledge her by name is a blessing that is sorely missed in most conversations. I pray that I'll not be afraid to speak the names of others who have gone home, if for no other reason than that I've learned those left behind want to hear those names.

She was here. She mattered. Ignoring that and never speaking about it may seem the easy road for some, and may avoid the possibility of uncomfortable memories or tears, but it is not the right solution. I've learned that now. Say her name. Talk about her.

As a pastor, I didn't know how to deal with death. What I thought was helpful wasn't. Words I thought so meaningful were of little help in my own grief. I won't say that they were of NO help, but the words were less helpful than other things, such as the hugs and the tears and the knowledge that others were praying. I pray that my words will be fewer the next time I'm called to the side of someone suffering pain and loss. I pray that my words will be fewer, and instead there will be more tears... more empathy... more embrace... more wordless care.

I need my brothers and sisters in Christ. As a pastor I have preached it forever, of course. Christians need to be actively engaged in their local church. I know it from my study of Scripture, and I have seen it countless times in my counseling of others. Church is important. The body of Christ is vital. We don't function well as believers outside of that community.

But this experience made it real to me. I was reminded that I desperately need the people of God in my life, and that I would be terribly diminished without it. Had I not had my church family... my brothers and sisters... during this time of crisis, I'm not sure I would have weathered it. They were there when I needed them (at least most of them). They brought words of encouragement, but they also brought so much more. Tears... touch... cards... phone calls... letters. There was food and provision brought to my home. The youth group came by and cleaned up the leaves in my yard. A brother mowed my lawn for me. In a myriad ways, my brothers and my sisters worked to show the love of Christ to me in this time of need, and I was and am reminded of the vital importance of the church in my life.

I realize that none of these lessons are earth shattering, but they are nonetheless a few of the things that have been driven into my heart from Beth's loss. And I expect that they are not the end of the things I'll learn.

I AM THANKFUL

What shall I render to the LORD For all His benefits toward me? (Psalms 116:12)

My brethren, count it all joy when you fall into various trials, (James 1:2)

in everything give thanks; for this is the will of God in Christ Jesus for you. (1 Thessalonians 5:18)

Not only that, but we rejoice in our sufferings, knowing that suffering produces endurance, and endurance produces character, and character produces hope, (Romans 5:3-4 ESV)

When I was going through the first steps of this journey of grief, thankfulness didn't play much of a part. Amazingly, some of it was there, but if I'm honest, I have to admit that the further I've gotten from the pain and suffering of those early days, the more the thankfulness part has grown. And now, many months removed, I can say that I'm truly thankful for some things.

I'm thankful that my wife knew Jesus Christ as her Savior. Of all the things I'm thankful for, this must come first. When I watched my wife die, there was not a moment of wondering whether she was in heaven or hell. She had told me repeatedly of how she came to believe the gospel of Jesus Christ in her teen years. I had watched her faithful and quiet testimony throughout our 35 years together. This was a woman who believed in the Savior, and was trusting in Him and Him alone for salvation. I never had to wonder whether my wife was saved or not, and for that I am eternally grateful. I know without a doubt that I will see her again, not because of some wishful thinking on my part, but because she was in every Biblical sense, a born again believer in Jesus Christ. Some weeks after the funeral had passed, I found the courage to pick up her Bible and leaf through it. Every page made me weep, for she had written so many things that spoke of her continued growth in Christ. But there was one note that I rejoiced to see even more than any other. She had written on the front page - "Born again - 1969."

How I thank God that she didn't leave me wondering... that I could rest in that sweet assurance... that there was no doubt.

I'm thankful that Beth made it to the end. She did not fall away at the end like so many "believers" do, but was serving Christ right up until her last day. As a matter of fact, with regard to her spiritual walk, she was running like Secretariat in the Belmont Stakes there at the end - picking up speed with each step.

I'm thankful she was spared the pain and suffering of age and disease. Loss is loss. Pain is pain. Separation is separation. No matter how we find ourselves losing a loved one, I'm certain it is a terrible experience. But having drawn near the bedside of so many believers who suffered long and died slowly, I have to admit a certain thankfulness that my sweet wife was spared this. I feel selfish writing it down, but I'm nonetheless, even if it is selfish, thankful that she was taken home so quickly and painlessly.

I'm thankful that she is freed from sin now. *For he who has died has been freed from sin. (Romans 6:7)* That enemy that we all struggle with all our lives is no longer even present for her. She has not even a single concern about it. It doesn't even exist. What joy this must be for her. And I rejoice for her in it.

I'm thankful for what God did in my life through her life. I am plainly not the person I was when I met her 35 years ago, but have been completely molded and changed by my relationship with her. Every time I eat food, visit a restaurant, listen to music, read a book, sit down in front of the television, go for a drive, plan a vacation... ANYTHING I do now I find is somehow a result of the way she and I used to do it. I am who I am because she was who she was, and she shared that with me. Sometimes it makes me sad. She and I loved Bob Evan's Restaurants. The first time I entered one alone, I nearly made a spectacle of myself with sadness. I could see her everywhere, because it was so clearly a thing that we had always done together. I ordered the same things I would have ordered had she been there with me. My routine was what she had made it. This same thing plays out every place I go and in every activity in which I engage. And though it does make me sad, I also am so thankful. I like the things about her that rubbed off on me. I'm thankful for what God did in my life through her life.

I'm thankful that when one dies their influence lives on. It lives on in all of those whom the deceased influenced in life. But in Beth's case, because she chose to donate her organs, it also lives on in those who physically benefited from her death through the receipt of those gifts. I'm blessed by that thought.

I'm thankful that God has brought me to and through this trial. God saw us through the trial with Joshua, and we rejoiced in His resource and grace. Now He has brought me to this ultimate moment... this greatest of losses... and I have seen that His grace was sufficient. "He giveth more grace" has been demonstrated to me in this crucible, and I have even greater hope and faith that that resource will be there for me no matter the trials that await in the future.

I PRAY

Then He spoke a parable to them, that men always ought to pray and not lose heart, (Luke 18:1)

I pray that her death will result in life. I pray that more souls will be saved somehow as a result. I pray for her family and friends who are still without Christ, and for whom she prayed and wept often. I pray for the kids in the youth group she started. She had the privilege to see some of them come to Jesus. May other seed she sowed but did not see sprout, germinate... blossom... grow... and reproduce.

I pray for increased fervor in my soul-winning efforts. I always recognized that she had greater fervency for reaching the lost with the gospel than I did. Now, may the suddenness of her death be a continuing goad to not slack, even for a minute. May the fact she finished strong spur me to do so, too.

I pray for Christ to return QUICKLY. I know this might seem a selfish prayer, but it is Biblical. *Even so, come, Lord Jesus! (Revelation 22:20)* I find myself praying it even more often now.

I pray for the reunion. This is redundant with the previous thought, I know. But I look forward to it so much more now. I always looked forward to seeing friends and relatives who've gone before, but now that SHE is there... that one to whom my soul is knit forever... I find the "looking forward to" has become a throbbing desire... a deep longing that occupies my thoughts. Oh how I pray for the day I see her again.

As I ponder that final prayer request, I cannot help but

think of Dr. Gary Habermas' testimony to Lee Strobel, after Gary's wife died of cancer in 1995. Brother Strobel included this in his wonderful book "The Case for Christ" and it fits so well with my experience now, and my prayers.

> I sat on our porch. My wife was upstairs dying. Except for a few weeks, she was home through it all. It was an awful time. This was the worst thing that could possibly happen. But do you know what was amazing? My students would call me - not just one but several of them - and say, "At a time like this, aren't you glad about the resurrection?" As sober as those circumstances were, I had to smile for two reasons. First, my students were trying to cheer me up with my own teaching. And second, it worked.
>
> As I would sit there, I'd picture Job, who went through all that terrible stuff and asked questions of God, but then God turned the tables and asked him a few questions.
>
> I knew if God were to come to me, I'd ask only one question: "Lord, why is Debbie up there in bed?" And I think God would respond by asking gently, "Gary, did I raise my Son from the dead?"
>
> I'd say, "Come on, Lord, I've written seven books on that topic! Of course he was raised from the dead. But I want to know about Debbie!"
>
> I think he'd keep coming back to the same question - "Did I raise my Son from the dead?" "Did I raise my Son from the dead?" - until I got his point: the Resurrection says that if Jesus was raised two thousand years ago, there's an answer to Debbie's death in 1995. And do you know what? It worked for me while I was sitting on the porch, and it still works today.

MY Grief Observed

It was a horribly emotional time for me, but I couldn't get around the fact that the Resurrection is the answer for her suffering. I still worried; I still wondered what I'd do raising four kids alone. But there wasn't a time when that truth didn't comfort me.

Losing my wife was the most painful experience I've ever had to face, but if the Resurrection could get me through that, it can get me through anything. It was good for 30 A.D., it's good for 1995, it's good for 1998, and it's good beyond that.

That's not some sermon, I believe that with all my heart. If there's a resurrection, there's a heaven. If Jesus was raised, Debbie was raised. And I will be someday, too.

Then I'll see them both.[5]

I pray for that day!

---

[5] Strobel, Lee, "The Case For Christ"

I CONTINUE

"Something quite unexpected has happened. It came this morning early. For various reasons, not in themselves at all mysterious, my heart was lighter than it had been for many weeks."[6]

"And now that I come to think of it, there's no practical problem before me at all. I know the two great commandments, and I'd better get on with them."[7]

Also the word of the LORD came to me, saying, "Son of man, behold, I take away from you the desire of your eyes with one stroke; yet you shall neither mourn nor weep, nor shall your tears run down. So I spoke to the people in the morning, and at evening my wife died; and the next morning I did as I was commanded. (Ezekiel 24:15-16, 18)

---

[6]Lewis, C.S., "A Grief Observed"

[7]Ibid.

It seemed impossible at first, but as time has marched on, so too has my life. I continue in the things I did before, just without her by my side. And I find myself slowly beginning to look to the future. It's a different future than what she and I had designed in our planning sessions together, but I know it is God's future and therefore good and right.

I recall conversations with my sweet wife about what she would want should this ever happen. Those conversations took place, even though I now realize we were never really aware of just how important they were. "I would not want you alone," was one of the things we both said to the other. And as the days go by and loneliness increases, I find myself thinking more and more of a future with someone else.

She... this beautiful part of my life that cannot ever be replaced... this soul mate who will forever be knit together with my soul... this sweetheart who will ever live in my heart, has graduated to heaven. I look forward to seeing her again. But each day I look a little more forward to seeing what the next chapter here holds. And nothing in that next chapter diminishes in any way what the previous chapters meant.

One day Saul of Tarsus met Jesus on the Damascus Road. It was a life altering event. Everything Saul had worked for and planned for his entire life was wiped out in an instant when he came face to face with the risen Jesus. He could have been embittered by that, I suppose. He could have concentrated on all the things he had always held dear and shouted his frustration at Jesus over their loss. Instead, He looked into the face of Jesus, and into the face of a completely changed future, and prayed the same prayer I pray now as I face my unknown future - "Lord, what would you have me to do?"

ADDENDUM

As mentioned in the opening paragraphs of this booklet, it was not my intention to write a Bible study or a doctrinal work. However, there is one truth from Scripture that needs to be shared. She would want it shared, if for no other reason than that she prayed for so many of her family and friends to know it and believe it.

I mentioned that I was thankful she had left me in no doubt about her soul. She was a Christian... a believer in the Lord Jesus Christ. She had been saved... born again... redeemed. She was forgiven and justified. And how that came to be in her life is what she would want shared.

In the last couple years of her life, Beth had started working on a book she hoped to publish. And after her death I began digging through the many pages she had written, intending to finish it for her. As a result of that effort, I came across a chapter she had written entitled, "What I Want My Family To Know." Here is an excerpt:

So what do I want my family to know?

1. My faith in Jesus Christ was the single most important thing in my life. Choosing Him to be my Savior was the best decision that I ever made.

2. I loved, adored, and cherished my husband. He was the only man that could turn my head... all the way around. He was my best friend.

3. My children were the light of my life. They were the best career I ever had. My job to bring them up in the fear and admonition of the Lord was a privilege that I didn't take lightly or carelessly.

4. My church work was my passion. There was never a grumble in my heart about serving the Lord in my local church.

5. I was successful at my secular job only because the Lord allowed me to be. He was the smart professional.

6. I had too many hobbies. Have fun cleaning out my craft room. It is packed full and waiting for you.

Now I know that most of the comments on that list were directed at her immediate family, and as such are precious mostly to them. But when I read that list and see that of all the things that she loved, she listed her relationship with Christ... her Christianity... her salvation FIRST, I know that she would want anybody reading this booklet to have that same assurance.

So I leave you with three simple truths from the Bible. This is how you, like Beth, can be saved and have the assurance that when your eyes close in death here, they will open there in heaven where you will live forever with the Lord. If you are already assured that you will go to heaven when you die, as Beth was, then you can stop reading now. But if you want to know more about how to become a Christian, please read these last few paragraphs.

You see - Jesus plainly stated that He is the only way to heaven. He said, *I am the way , the truth, and the life. No man comes to the Father but by me. (John 14:6)* There are not many ways to God. There is only one way, and that is through Jesus Christ.

The Bible is the guidebook explaining that one way, and here is a simplified outline of what it teaches about how to become a Christian:

Admit that you have sinned. *All have sinned and fall short of the glory of God. (Romans 3:23)*

Believe that Jesus died for you. *Believe in the Lord Jesus, and you will be saved. (Acts 16:31) For God so loved the world that he gave his one and only Son, that whoever believes in him shall not perish but have eternal life. (John 3:16)*

Call upon Him. *That if you confess with your mouth, 'Jesus is Lord,' and believe in your heart that God raised him from the dead, you will be saved. For it is with your heart that you believe and are justified, and it is with your mouth that you confess and are saved. (Romans 10:9-10) For whoever calls on the name of the Lord shall be saved. (Romans 10:13)*

I pray, as Beth prayed, that you will think through those three simple truths, and act upon them... that you will come to know the Jesus she knew and loved, so that when the day comes where someone you love is faced with grieving your loss, they will not have to wonder.

Read those verses again if they haven't sunk in. And then pray, and ask for the salvation Christ wants you to have.

Salvation is the greatest gift you will ever receive. And your loved ones knowing that you are saved, is the greatest gift you can ever give them, for when the time comes where they are in the midst of their grief observed, they will be able to smile through that grief, knowing you are just fine with Christ.

ABOUT THE AUTHOR

William E. Johnson is a follower of Jesus Christ. He was born again at age 12, served in his local church throughout his teen years, and then entered formal Bible College training as a young adult. Bill has served as pastor of 2 small churches, as well as in a variety of other roles, including minister of music, deacon, and associate pastor.

His passion is the Bible. Whether via preaching or writing, he desires to share the good news of God's Word and the gospel of Jesus Christ to as many as will hear and read.

Additional books and booklets, both paperback and eBook, are available at:

http://amazon.com/author/johnsonacres

Printed in Great Britain
by Amazon